The Renaissance Bingo Book

A COMPLETE BINGO GAME IN A BOOK

Madonna of the Magnificat
By Sandro Botticelli

Written By Rebecca Stark

TITLE: The Renaissance Bingo
AUTHOR: Rebecca Stark

ISBN 978-0-87386-482-4

Educational Books 'n' Bingo

Printed in the U.S.A.

BINGO
Directions

1. Cut apart the sheets of heavy-stock paper which contain the call cards with topics and clues. Copies of these sheets are also provided on plain paper for your convenience. You may want to use them to review with your students.

2. Pass out one bingo card per student. There are enough for a class of 30.

3. Pass out markers. You may use pennies, beans, or any other small items of your choice.

4. Decide whether or not you will require the entire card to be filled. Requiring the entire card to be filled provides a better review. However, if you have a short time to fill, you may prefer to have them do the just the border or some other format. Tell the class before you begin what is required.

5. There are 50 topics. Read the list before you begin. If there are any topics that have not been covered in class, you may want to read to the students the topic and clues before you begin.

6. There is a blank space in the middle of each card. You can instruct the students to use it as a free space or you can write in answers to cover topics not included. Of course, in this case you would create your own clues. (Templates provided.)

7. Shuffle the cards and place them in a pile. Two or three clues are provided for each topic. If you plan to play the game with the same group more than once, you might want to choose a different clue for each game. If not, you may choose to use both clues.

8. Be sure to keep the cards you have used for the present game in a separate pile. When a student calls, "Bingo," he or she will have to verify that the correct answers are on his or her card AND that the markers were placed in response to the proper questions. Pull out the cards that are on the student's card keeping them in the order they were used in the game. Read each clue as it was given and ask the student to identify the correct answer from his or her card.

9. If the student has the correct answers on the card AND has shown that they were marked in response to the *correct questions,* then that student is the winner and the game is over. If the student does not have the correct answers on the card OR he or she marked the answers in response to *the wrong questions,* then the game continues until there is a proper winner.

10. If you want to play again, reshuffle the cards and begin again.

Have fun!

VARIATION: You may want to ask for a volunteer to give the correct answer after each clue is given.

TERMS

The Book of the Courtier

Tycho Brahe

Filippo Brunelleschi

Guiliano Bugiardini

John Cabot

caravel

Baldassare Castiglione

city-state(s)

Christopher Columbus

Nicolaus Copernicus

Counter Reformation

Vasco da Gama

Leonardo da Vinci

doge

dome(s)

Duomo

English

Florence

fresco

Galileo Galilei

The Golden Book

guild(s)

gunpowder

Johannes Gutenberg

heliocentric

Henry Hudson

humanism

Johannes Kepler

Martin Luther

Niccolo Machiavelli

Ferdinand Magellan

Mannerism

Christopher Marlowe

Medici

Michelangelo

Isaac Newton

patron

perspective

Francis Petrarch

Prince Henry the Navigator

Raphael Sanzio

Reformation

Renaissance

William Shakespeare

Sistene Chapel

sonnet

tapestries

Titian

Jan van Eyck

Venice

Note: Some of the names have alternate spellings not shown here.

The Book of the Courtier 1. It was written by Baldassare Castiglione over the course of many years. 2. It is organized as a series of conversations between the courtiers of the Duke of Urbino as they describe the perfect gentleman of the court.	**Tycho Brahe** 1. This Danish nobleman is credited with the most accurate astronomical observations of his time. 2. This astronomer's data was used by his assistant, Johannes Kepler, to derive the laws of planetary motion.
Filippo Brunelleschi 1. He is best known for designing the dome of the Florence Cathedral. 2. This Italian architect and engineer is known for the Duomo of the Basilica di Santa Maria del Fiore in Florence.	**Guiliano Bugiardini** 1. Some of his best known works were three separate pieces, all titled _Virgin and Child with the Infant Saint John the Baptist._ 2. This late Renaissance Italian painter was associated with the Mannerist style of painting.
John Cabot 1. This Italian explorer sailed for England; his real name was Giovanni Caboto. 2. He was the first European since the Vikings to explore the mainland of North America and the first to search for the Northwest Passage.	**caravel** 1. A ___ is a small, highly maneuverable sailing ship. 2. This sailing ship was developed in the 15th century by the Portuguese.
Baldassare Castiglione 1. This Renaissance author is best known for _The Book of the Courtier._ 2. Raphael painted a portrait of this Italian High Renaissance gentleman.	**city-state(s)** 1. During the Renaissance, Italy was a collection of ___. 2. A ___ is a sovereign state consisting of an independent city and its surrounding territory.
Christopher Columbus 1. This Italian explorer sailed for Spain in 1492. 2. Although he was not first the European to discover the New World, his voyages were the first to lead to real contact with the native people.	**Nicolaus Copernicus** 1. This Polish astronomer was the first to formulate a heliocentric model of the universe. 2. Galileo was put under house arrest because he supported the heliocentric theory of ___.

The Renaissance Bingo

Counter Revolution	**Vasco da Gama**
1. This reform movement within the Roman Catholic Church arose in 16th-century Europe in response to the Protestant Reformation.	1. This Portuguese explorer discovered an ocean route from Portugal to the East.
2. It was a period of Catholic revival in 16th-century Europe.	2. In November 1497 his expedition rounded Africa's Cape of Good Hope and continued on to India.
Leonardo da Vinci	**doge**
1. His drawing entitled *The Vitruvian Man* is an example of his deep interest in proportion.	1. It was the name given to the chief magistrate of Venice.
2. His painting *The Last Supper* is the most reproduced painting of all time.	2. Only the aristocrats of Venice could vote for this official.
dome(s)	**Duomo**
1. Along with arches, vaults, and columns, ___ were a common feature of Renaissance architecture.	1. It is the Italian word for "dome."
2. This structural element of architecture resembles the hollow upper half of a sphere.	2. The dome of the Basilica di Santa Maria del Fiore in Florence is so famous that it is often referred to simply as Il ___.
English	**Florence**
1. Elizabethan was one form of ___ architecture.	1. The Renaissance is said to have begun in this Italian city-state.
2. Jacobean was another form of ___ architecture.	2. Banking was very important to this Italian city-state. The Medicis were an important banking family here.
fresco	**Galileo Galilei**
1. It is the art of painting on fresh, moist plaster with pigments dissolved in water.	1. Using telescopes he had built, he discovered four of Jupiter's moons and saw craters on the moon.
2. *The Last Judgment*, by Michelangelo, is a ___ on the altar wall of the Sistine Chapel.	2. He was put under house arrest for supporting the heliocentric theory of the universe put forth by Copernicus.

The Renaissance Bingo

The Golden Book 1. During the Renaissance ___ was a formal directory of nobles in Venice. 2. During the Renaissance, only those listed in ___ could vote for the doge.	**guild(s)** 1. It is an association of craftsmen in a particular trade. 2. There were 12 artist ___ that regulated the trades in Florence.
gunpowder 1. ___ began to be used in Europe during the Renaissance. It greatly changed the way wars were fought. 2. ___ was probably used for the first time in Europe during the Battle of Crécy in 1346.	**Johannes Gutenberg** 1. He invented the movable-type printing press. 2. His invention meant that books could be produced in large quantities in a short period of time.
heliocentric 1. This adjective describes the astronomical model in which the Earth and planets revolve around the sun. 2. Copernicus was the first to formulate a ___ model of the universe.	**Henry Hudson** 1. This English explorer and navigator explored northeastern North America. A river, strait and bay are all named for him. 2. His ship was called the *Half Moon.*
humanism 1. Renaissance ___ was marked by a renewed interest in the classics, including literary, scientific, political and artistic works. 2. ___ refers to the social philosophy and intellectual and literary trends of the Renaissance.	**Johannes Kepler** 1. This German mathematician and astronomer was the first to correctly explain planetary motion. 2. He is best known for his laws of planetary motion.
Martin Luther 1. This German monk was a key figure in the Protestant Reformation. 2. In 1517 he nailed his *Ninety-five Theses of Contention* to the Wittenberg Church door.	**Niccolo Machiavelli** 1. "The end justifies the means" is attributed to this Italian historian, philosopher, and writer. 2. He was the author of *The Prince,* a political treatise.

Ferdinand Magellan 1. His expedition was the first to sail from the Atlantic Ocean into the Pacific Ocean. 2. Although he himself did not complete the entire voyage, his expedition made the first circumnavigation of the Earth.	**Mannerism** 1. This artistic style predominated in Italy from the end of the High Renaissance to the beginnings of the Baroque style around 1590. 2. This artistic style originated as a reaction to the harmonious classicism.
Christopher Marlowe 1. This English Renaissance author greatly influenced William Shakespeare. 2. He is probably best known for his work commonly called *Doctor Faustus.*	**Medici** 1. This banking family was a political dynasty in Florence and a patron of the arts. 2. Cosimo and Lorenzo were two prominent members of this Florentine family.
Michelangelo 1. Commonly called by his first name, this great Renaissance artist painted the ceiling of the Sistene Chapel. 2. His sculpture of David is considered a masterpiece.	**Isaac Newton** 1. This English physicist and mathematician is known for his law of universal gravitation and the 3 laws of motion. 2. He showed the consistency between Kepler's laws of planetary motion and his theory of gravitation.
patron 1. A wealthy or influential supporter of an artist or writer is called a ___. 2. Renaissance artists who did not have a ___ could not survive.	**perspective** 1. The Italian painter Tommaso Masaccio is known for his use of ___, which gave an illusion of 3 dimensions. 2. ___ is a technique of depicting spatial relationships on a flat surface.
Francis Petrarch 1. The Italian sonnet form in which the 14 lines are divided into an octet and a sestet is named for him. 2. The real name of this Italian Renaissance poet was Francesco Petrarca.	**Prince Henry the Navigator** 1. Although not himself an explorer, he sponsored many sailing expeditions. 2. This patron of explorers helped begin the Great Age of Discovery.

© Barbara M Peller

Raphael Sanzio 1. Better known by his first name, along with Michelangelo and Leonardo da Vinci, this Italian artist was a great master of the High Renaissance. 2. His fresco The *School of Athens* is in the Vatican.	**Reformation** 1. This 16th-century schism within Western Christianity was initiated by Martin Luther and others. 2. It began in 1517 when Martin Luther nailed his *Ninety Theses* to a church door in Wittenberg, Germany.
Renaissance 1. This cultural movement spanned the period roughly from the 14th to the 17th century. 2. It began in Italy in the mid-14th century and spread throughout Europe.	**William Shakespeare** 1. This English poet and playwright is widely regarded as the greatest writer in the English language. 2. This English poet and playwright wrote 37 plays and 154 sonnets.
Sistene Chapel 1. Located within the Vatican, its ceiling was painted by Michelangelo. 2. Its side walls were decorated with frescoes by the greatest Italian Renaissance artists.	**sonnet** 1. The Italian, or Petrarchan, ___ has an octave and a sestet. 2. The English, or Shakespearean, ___ has 3 quatrains of alternating rhyme and a couplet.
tapestries 1. These heavy pieces of fabric with a woven picture were often used as wall hangings. 2. The Netherlands was known for cloth production and its ___ were exported all over Europe.	**Titian** 1. Tiziano Vecellio, better known as ___, is known above all for his remarkable use of color. 2. ___ red is reddish-gold; it is named for the artist who used this hair color in many of his works.
Jan van Eyck 1. This Flemish painter is known for his innovative use of oil paints. He was one of the most significant Northern European painters of the 15th century. 2. His *Portrait of a Man in a Turban* might have been a self-portrait.	**Venice** 1. Like Florence, this Italian city had the economy to support art and artists. 2. Bookmaking flourished in this Italian city during the fifteenth century.

Additional Terms

Choose as many other terms as you would like and write them in the squares. Repeat each as desired. Cut out the squares and randomly distribute them to the class. Instruct the students to place the square on the center space of their card.

Clues for
Additional Terms

Write two or three clues for each of your additional terms.

_____

1.

2.

3.

_____

1.

2.

3.

_____

1.

2.

3.

_____

1.

2.

3.

_____

1.

2.

3.

_____

1.

2.

3.

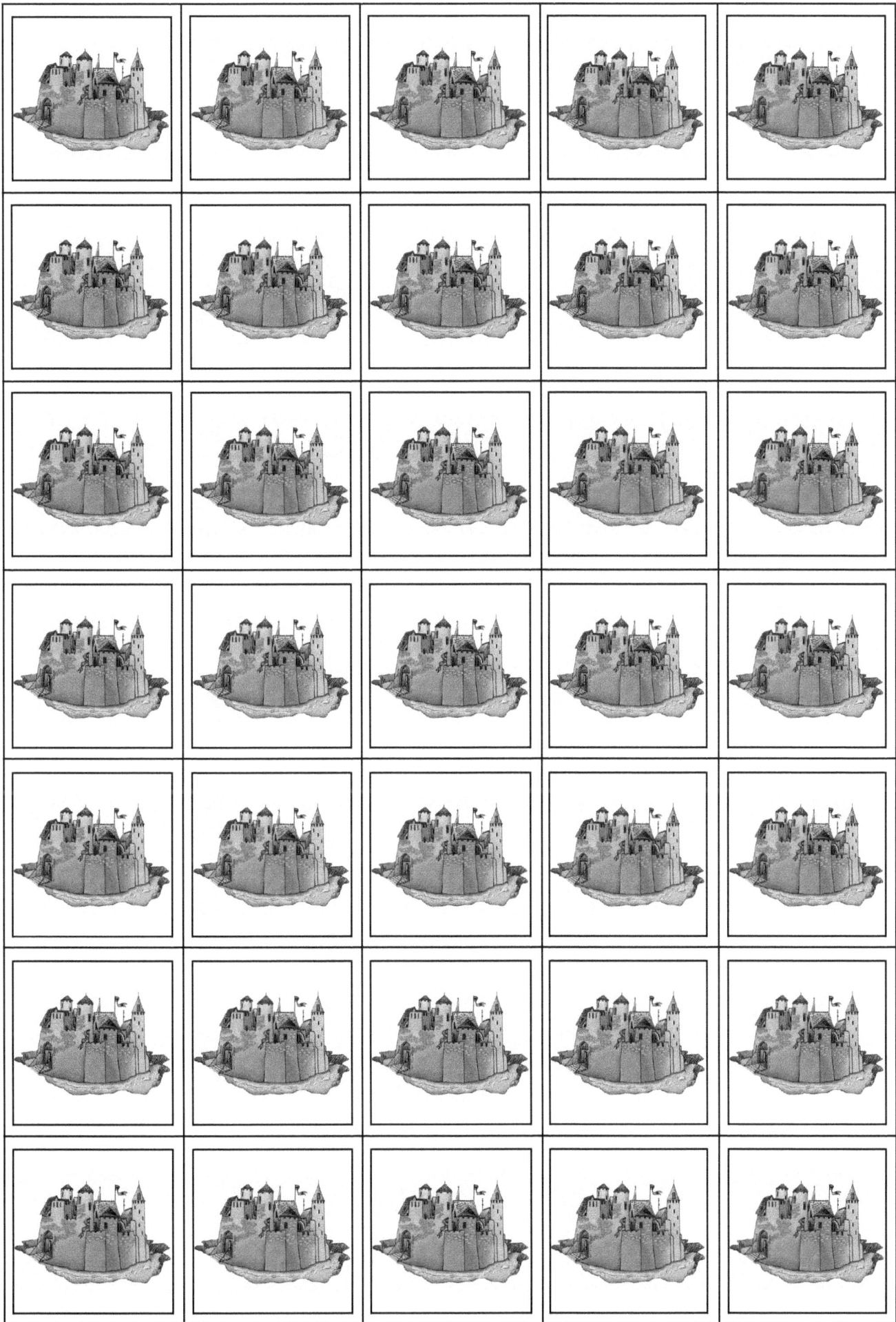

The Renaissance Bingo

guild(s)	Galileo Galilei	gunpowder	Venice	tapestries
Christopher Columbus	Tycho Brahe	Jan van Eyck	Martin Luther	*The Golden Book*
Reformation	Isaac Newton		Johannes Gutenberg	Christopher Marlow
sonnet	*The Book of the Courtier*	Francis Petrarch	William Shakespeare	heliocentric
Henry Hudson	Nicolaus Copernicus	Vasco da Gama	Florence	fresco

The Renaissance Bingo: Card No. 1

The Renaissance Bingo

sonnet	Francis Petrarch	Martin Luther	William Shakespeare	Reformation
Nicolaus Copernicus	Tycho Brahe	John Cabot	Galileo Galilei	Niccolo Machiavelli
The Book of the Courtier	Jan van Eyck		Raphael Sanzio	Filippo Brunelleschi
Isaac Newton	perspective	Henry Hudson	English	humanism
Florence	Christopher Columbus	Vasco da Gama	Ferdinand Magellan	gunpowder

The Renaissance

Bingo

The Renaissance Bingo

Isaac Newton	Raphael Sanzio	Henry Hudson	Christopher Columbus	gunpowder
Johannes Kepler	Baldassare Castiglione	Galileo Galilei	Michelangelo	Reformation
Johannes Gutenberg	English		tapestries	Venice
Francis Petrarch	Duomo	Jan van Eyck	Vasco da Gama	John Cabot
dome(s)	fresco	Medici	Florence	Christopher Marlow

The Renaissance Bingo

fresco	tapestries	*The Book of the Courtier*	Baldassare Castiglione	Christopher Columbus
Johannes Kepler	Francis Petrarch	John Cabot	Leonardo da Vinci	Tycho Brahe
Renaissance	Christopher Marlow		doge	Counter Revolution
The Golden Book	Raphael Sanzio	guild(s)	Ferdinand Magellan	dome(s)
Martin Luther	Vasco da Gama	patron	Isaac Newton	Johannes Gutenberg

The Renaissance Bingo

Filippo Brunelleschi	Raphael Sanzio	humanism	Renaissance	Christopher Marlow
William Shakespeare	*The Book of the Courtier*	dome(s)	Galileo Galilei	Reformation
Michelangelo	John Cabot		Baldassare Castiglione	Leonardo da Vinci
Vasco da Gama	Henry Hudson	Ferdinand Magellan	Medici	Johannes Gutenberg
heliocentric	Francis Petrarch	guild(s)	patron	gunpowder

The Renaissance Bingo

sonnet	Renaissance	humanism	Michelangelo	Henry Hudson
heliocentric	Martin Luther	Baldassare Castiglione	*The Book of the Courtier*	Raphael Sanzio
perspective	Nicolaus Copernicus		Leonardo da Vinci	Francis Petrarch
English	Prince Henry the Navigator	Isaac Newton	Ferdinand Magellan	*The Golden Book*
fresco	Jan van Eyck	Vasco da Gama	Christopher Columbus	Florence

The Renaissance Bingo

guild(s)	Raphael Sanzio	Counter Revolution	doge	Martin Luther
heliocentric	gunpowder	Nicolaus Copernicus	Tycho Brahe	Johannes Kepler
humanism	Venice		Leonardo da Vinci	Guiliano Bugiardini
Isaac Newton	English	Reformation	sonnet	perspective
Vasco da Gama	Christopher Columbus	Ferdinand Magellan	Medici	Filippo Brunelleschi

The Renaissance Bingo

Johannes Gutenberg	Raphael Sanzio	caravel	William Shakespeare	Guiliano Bugiardini
Johannes Kepler	Renaissance	Michelangelo	Christopher Marlow	Baldassare Castiglione
Reformation	Mannerism		gunpowder	tapestries
Florence	Isaac Newton	sonnet	dome(s)	English
Jan van Eyck	Vasco da Gama	Medici	*The Book of the Courtier*	heliocentric

The Renaissance Bingo

Leonardo da Vinci	Martin Luther	Nicolaus Copernicus	Reformation	Christopher Marlow
dome(s)	Renaissance	Johannes Gutenberg	*The Book of the Courtier*	gunpowder
Niccolo Machiavelli	guild(s)		Tycho Brahe	caravel
Guiliano Bugiardini	fresco	Henry Hudson	doge	Counter Revolution
English	Ferdinand Magellan	John Cabot	sonnet	tapestries

The Renaissance Bingo

sonnet	William Shakespeare	Baldassare Castiglione	Michelangelo	patron
Christopher Marlow	Guiliano Bugiardini	Galileo Galilei	Tycho Brahe	gunpowder
Mannerism	Raphael Sanzio		Venice	perspective
Henry Hudson	*The Golden Book*	dome(s)	Ferdinand Magellan	Niccolo Machiavelli
city-state(s)	heliocentric	humanism	fresco	Johannes Gutenberg

The Renaissance Bingo

Filippo Brunelleschi	Raphael Sanzio	*The Book of the Courtier*	dome(s)	heliocentric
caravel	Niccolo Machiavelli	doge	Leonardo da Vinci	Galileo Galilei
Johannes Kepler	Renaissance		humanism	Nicolaus Copernicus
city-state(s)	Reformation	Ferdinand Magellan	Christopher Columbus	sonnet
John Cabot	Vasco da Gama	guild(s)	Medici	Martin Luther

The Renaissance Bingo

Martin Luther	tapestries	Niccolo Machiavelli	William Shakespeare	Leonardo da Vinci
Nicolaus Copernicus	Jan van Eyck	Renaissance	Medici	Tycho Brahe
guild(s)	Counter Revolution		Christopher Marlow	Michelangelo
Vasco da Gama	English	gunpowder	sonnet	Johannes Kepler
Raphael Sanzio	caravel	Mannerism	John Cabot	Guiliano Bugiardini

The Renaissance Bingo

city-state(s)	tapestries	Filippo Brunelleschi	Niccolo Machiavelli	Christopher Marlow
Renaissance	caravel	Raphael Sanzio	Leonardo da Vinci	perspective
William Shakespeare	Baldassare Castiglione		Nicolaus Copernicus	Counter Revolution
Johannes Gutenberg	Ferdinand Magellan	Guiliano Bugiardini	Mannerism	sonnet
Vasco da Gama	*The Golden Book*	Medici	guild(s)	doge

The Renaissance Bingo

Christopher Columbus	Renaissance	*The Book of the Courtier*	Leonardo da Vinci	city-state(s)
Guiliano Bugiardini	guild(s)	Niccolo Machiavelli	Tycho Brahe	Raphael Sanzio
dome(s)	Venice		humanism	John Cabot
The Golden Book	Ferdinand Magellan	Mannerism	Baldassare Castiglione	Filippo Brunelleschi
Vasco da Gama	Michelangelo	perspective	heliocentric	Johannes Gutenberg

The Renaissance Bingo

doge	Leonardo da Vinci	*The Book of the Courtier*	Martin Luther	William Shakespeare
Filippo Brunelleschi	humanism	Galileo Galilei	Renaissance	dome(s)
Christopher Marlow	guild(s)		Reformation	gunpowder
Vasco da Gama	Niccolo Machiavelli	caravel	Ferdinand Magellan	city-state(s)
heliocentric	English	Medici	patron	Nicolaus Copernicus

The Renaissance Bingo

Baldassare Castiglione	Niccolo Machiavelli	caravel	patron	Prince Henry the Navigator
Michelangelo	perspective	Counter Revolution	Johannes Kepler	Venice
city-state(s)	tapestries		Christopher Marlow	Nicolaus Copernicus
Isaac Newton	Guiliano Bugiardini	Vasco da Gama	doge	sonnet
dome(s)	Titian	Medici	English	Raphael Sanzio

The Renaissance Bingo

city-state(s)	Sistene Chapel	Duomo	Niccolo Machiavelli	Christopher Columbus
doge	dome(s)	Ferdinand Magellan	Venice	Counter Revolution
Leonardo da Vinci	sonnet		Titian	caravel
fresco	heliocentric	Johannes Gutenberg	*The Book of the Courtier*	perspective
Henry Hudson	John Cabot	Martin Luther	William Shakespeare	tapestries

The Renaissance Bingo

gunpowder	Mannerism	Guiliano Bugiardini	dome(s)	Michelangelo
Raphael Sanzio	city-state(s)	Henry Hudson	Christopher Marlow	John Cabot
Leonardo da Vinci	perspective		Duomo	patron
fresco	Galileo Galilei	Ferdinand Magellan	sonnet	humanism
Titian	Niccolo Machiavelli	*The Book of the Courtier*	Sistene Chapel	Filippo Brunelleschi

The Renaissance Bingo

The Renaissance Bingo

Christopher Marlow	Filippo Brunelleschi	Niccolo Machiavelli	caravel	Mannerism
doge	William Shakespeare	patron	Martin Luther	Venice
Sistene Chapel	Christopher Columbus		Tycho Brahe	gunpowder
humanism	Titian	Henry Hudson	English	Duomo
Reformation	Prince Henry the Navigator	heliocentric	Johannes Gutenberg	Medici

The Renaissance Bingo

Bartholomew		Pope Brunelleschi	Christopher Marlow	
Venice	Martin Luther		William Shakespeare	doge
gunpowder	Vasco da Gama		Christopher Columbus	Sistine Chapel
Europe	England	Henry Hudson	Titian	humanism
Medici	Johannes Gutenberg	heliocentric	Prince Henry the Navigator	Reformation

The Renaissance Bingo

Mannerism	Sistene Chapel	William Shakespeare	Niccolo Machiavelli	Tycho Brahe
Baldassare Castiglione	Nicolaus Copernicus	Johannes Kepler	Henry Hudson	Michelangelo
tapestries	Counter Revolution		Isaac Newton	Galileo Galilei
fresco)	Johannes Gutenberg	Florence	English	Titian
Francis Petrarch	Jan van Eyck	Prince Henry the Navigator	sonnet	Duomo

The Renaissance Bingo

doge	Filippo Brunelleschi	Johannes Kepler	Niccolo Machiavelli	*The Golden Book*
tapestries	Duomo	Guiliano Bugiardini	caravel	guild(s)
perspective	heliocentric		Sistene Chapel	*The Book of the Courtier*
Henry Hudson	Martin Luther	Titian	fresco	Johannes Gutenberg
Isaac Newton	Prince Henry the Navigator	Medici	city-state(s)	English

The Renaissance Bingo

Reformation	humanism	Duomo	Renaissance	city-state(s)
Michelangelo	William Shakespeare	gunpowder	caravel	Tycho Brahe
Guiliano Bugiardini	Venice		guild(s)	Counter Revolution
Titian	fresco	English	Galileo Galilei	Christopher Columbus
Prince Henry the Navigator	John Cabot	Sistene Chapel	perspective	Johannes Kepler

The Renaissance Bingo

Baldassare Castiglione	Sistene Chapel	Martin Luther	Renaissance	Medici
Filippo Brunelleschi	Mannerism	heliocentric	doge	Galileo Galilei
humanism	city-state(s)		Florence	guild(s)
perspective	Prince Henry the Navigator	Titian	John Cabot	English
The Golden Book	Johannes Gutenberg	Jan van Eyck	Henry Hudson	Duomo

The Renaissance Bingo

Baldassare Castiglione	Mannerism	Christopher Columbus	Sistene Chapel	caravel
Christopher Marlow	Medici	Johannes Kepler	Michelangelo	guild(s)
Counter Revolution	patron		city-state(s)	perspective
The Golden Book	Florence	Titian	John Cabot	tapestries
Francis Petrarch	Isaac Newton	Prince Henry the Navigator	William Shakespeare	Jan van Eyck

The Renaissance Bingo

Isaac Newton	Johannes Kepler	Sistene Chapel	*The Book of the Courtier*	Duomo
Galileo Galilei	*The Golden Book*	doge	Baldassare Castiglione	Tycho Brahe
tapestries	caravel		Florence	Titian
patron	fresco	Jan van Eyck	Prince Henry the Navigator	Venice
Medici	Christopher Columbus	Guiliano Bugiardini	dome(s)	Francis Petrarch

The Renaissance Bingo

Duomo	Sistene Chapel	Florence	Michelangelo	patron
Henry Hudson	William Shakespeare	caravel	Mannerism	Baldassare Castiglione
The Golden Book	humanism		Venice	Isaac Newton
city-state(s)	Renaissance	fresco	Prince Henry the Navigator	Titian
Counter Revolution	dome(s)	*The Book of the Courtier*	Jan van Eyck	Francis Petrarch

The Renaissance Bingo

Florence	Guiliano Bugiardini	Sistene Chapel	Mannerism	Nicolaus Copernicus
The Golden Book	humanism	doge	Titian	Tycho Brahe
Ferdinand Magellan	Jan van Eyck		Prince Henry the Navigator	Isaac Newton
patron	Filippo Brunelleschi	Johannes Kepler	Francis Petrarch	Galileo Galilei
city-state(s)	Venice	Duomo	Reformation	Counter Revolution

The Renaissance Bingo

Christopher Marlow	Mannerism	sonnet	Sistene Chapel	Guiliano Bugiardini
Nicolaus Copernicus	Duomo	Florence	Henry Hudson	Venice
Jan van Eyck	perspective		patron	Michelangelo
Counter Revolution	Reformation	heliocentric	Prince Henry the Navigator	Titian
Renaissance	Leonardo da Vinci	city-state(s)	Francis Petrarch	*The Golden Book*

The Renaissance Bingo

Duomo	Mannerism	patron	doge	Leonardo da Vinci
The Golden Book	Henry Hudson	Johannes Kepler	Counter Revolution	Reformation
tapestries	Florence		Tycho Brahe	Sistene Chapel
Nicolaus Copernicus	fresco	gunpowder	Prince Henry the Navigator	Titian
Baldassare Castiglione	caravel	Francis Petrarch	Filippo Brunelleschi	Jan van Eyck

The Renaissance Bingo

Christopher Columbus	Sistene Chapel	Michelangelo	Leonardo da Vinci	tapestries
Galileo Galilei	patron	humanism	Venice	Tycho Brahe
Francis Petrarch	John Cabot		Counter Revolution	Johannes Kepler
The Golden Book	Filippo Brunelleschi	Mannerism	Prince Henry the Navigator	Florence
fresco	Martin Luther	Jan van Eyck	Duomo	gunpowder

www.ingramcontent.com/pod-product-compliance
Lightning Source LLC
LaVergne TN
LVHW061339060426
835511LV00014B/2011